© 2024 Newbee Publication
All rights Reserved

Scan QR code for more Publications

No part of this publication may be reproduced, distributed, or transmitted in any form or by any means, including photocopying, recording, or other electronic or mechanical methods, without the prior written permission of the publisher

Once upon a time, in a lush green forest, there lived a young turtle named Tiki

Tiki was friendly and kind, but he found it hard to share his toys with others.

One sunny day, while playing with his colourful toys by the riverbank, Bobo Bunny, Sisi Squirrel, and Pupo Parrot came along.

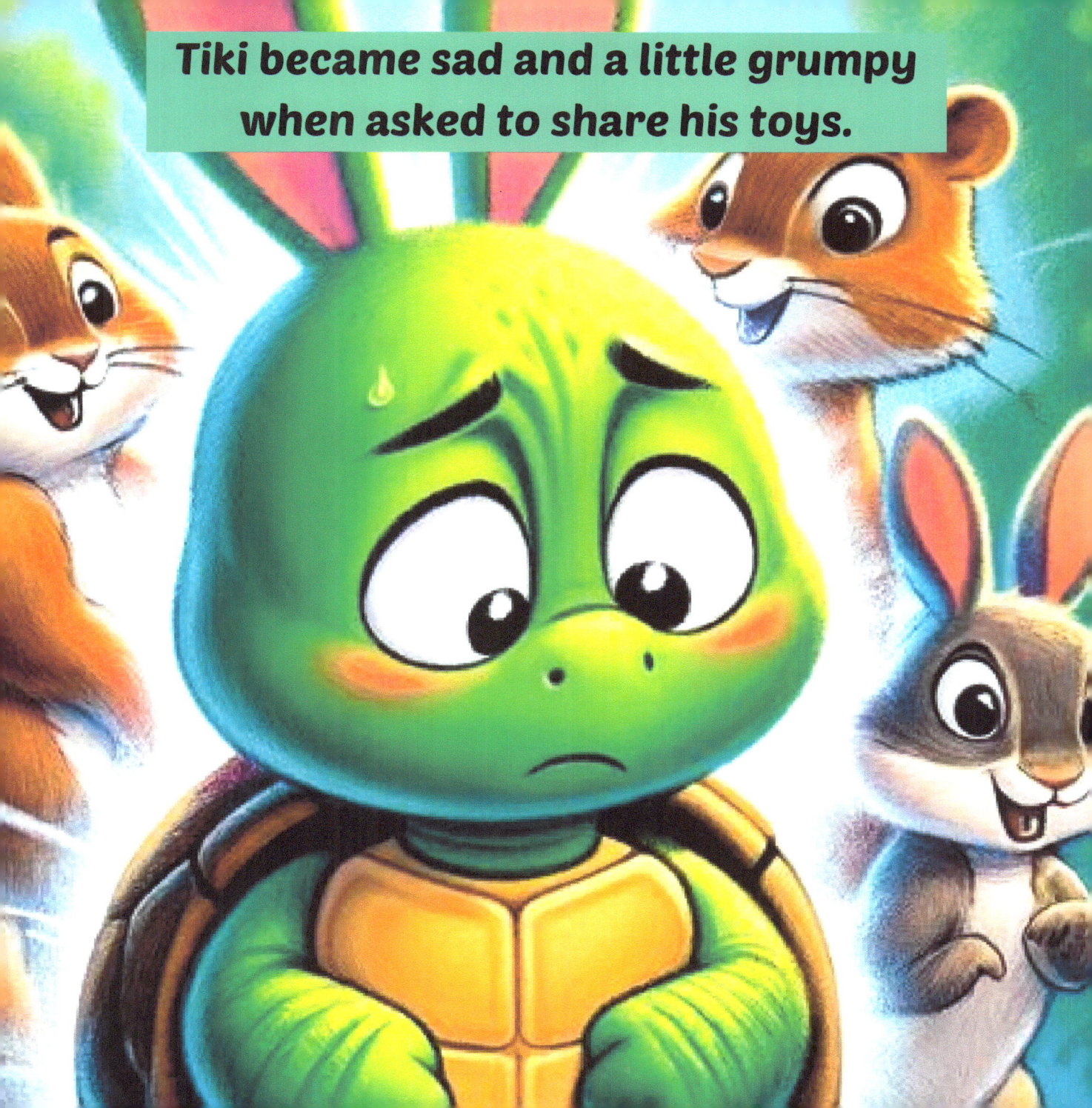

However, Tiki felt uneasy about sharing and

decided to play by himself.

While playing alone, a block slipped from his grasp and rolled down into a narrow, dark hole under a tree.

Tiki tried but was so scared of dark

But the hole was too dark and deep for him to retrieve it.

Seeing Tiki sad, Bobo Bunny, Sisi Squirrel, and Pupo Parrot approached him. "What's wrong, Tiki?"

They asked. Tiki explained his problem, and immediately, his friends sprang into action.

Bobo Bunny attempted to jump in, but the hole was too deep.

Together, they worked in harmony to retrieve the block.

He realized how important his friends were and decided to share all his toys with them.

As they built colourful structures together

Then, they built grand castles and towers, laughing and creating wonderful memories.

Tiki learned that sharing not only solves problems but also makes every moment more enjoyable.

Tiki realized playing together is much more fun.

While they were playing with a red ball

Suddenly, a gust of wind carried their red ball towards the river.

Tiki learned that sharing toys makes everyone happy, so he asked his friends to come over for a play day!"

The day arrived, and Tiki's friends came to play

Tiki shared all his toys with his friends.

The forest was filled with sounds of laughter and joy as the friends shared everything they had,

Creating a bond of friendship that would last forever.

Great job! You finished the story and earned 5 golden stars.

Remember, sharing is fun!"

www.ingramcontent.com/pod-product-compliance
Lightning Source LLC
Chambersburg PA
CBHW050748110526
44591CB00002B/16